Around the Churches
of
EXETER

Walter Jacobson

GW00585094

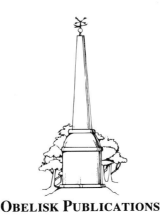

OBELISK PUBLICATIONS

ALSO BY THE AUTHOR

Around the Churches of East Devon, *Walter Jacobson*

OTHER BOOKS ABOUT EXETER

The Great Little Exeter Book, *Chips Barber*
The Ghosts of Exeter, *Sally and Chips Barber*
Beautiful Exeter, *Chips Barber*
Exploring Exeter, *Jean Maun*
Topsham Past and Present, *Chips Barber*
An Alphington Album, *Pauline Aplin and Jeanne Gaskell*
Exeter City – A File of Fascinating Football Facts, *Mike Blackstone*
Ian Jubb's Exeter Collection
An Exeter Boyhood, *Frank Retter*
The Lost City of Exeter, *Chips Barber*
Pinhoe of Yesteryear, *Chips Barber*
Pinhoe of Yesteryear, Part II, *Chips Barber*
Heavitree of Yesteryear, *Chips Barber*

We have over 150 Devon-based titles – for a list of current books please write to us at 2 Church Hill, Pinhoe, Exeter, EX4 9ER telephone (01392) 468556.

Acknowledgements

All photographs supplied by Walter Jacobson, Chips Barber and Mrs Higgins. Thanks to the Devon Historic Churches Trust, the *Express & Echo*, and Gemini AM.

First published in 1998 by
Obelisk Publications, 2 Church Hill, Pinhoe, Exeter, Devon
Designed by Chips and Sally Barber
Typeset by Sally Barber
Printed in Great Britain by
Greenhill Press

CONTENTS

INTRODUCTION

EXETER Cathedral's well documented beauty and history win immediate attention from newcomers to Devon, and rightly so. Clus-tered around the Mother Church are the churches of the city, representing various denominations, and they, too, are places of restful beauty, each with a fascinating story to tell. Some of these churches in and around Exeter are the subject of this publication.

In writing a series of articles first published in the *Express and Echo* and later broadcast on local radio – at the request of the Devon Historic Churches Trust – I was greatly helped with the fund of information made available by the West Country Studies Library and the Exeter Cathedral Library and the records gathered by members of individual churches over the years. This book is a sequel to my *Around the Churches of East Devon.*

What I have selected from this wealth of material is mainly of human interest, and the conclusion must be that the people who built, decorated, and worshipped in these fas-cinating buildings were not so very different from ourselves.

The illustrations in this book include many old picture postcard views. As I have not highlighted any of the changes which have occurred since they were taken I will leave it to you to discover for yourself what they might be. A little bit of mystery or an element of surprise always adds a bit of spice!

As a journalist, amateur historian, and sentimental clergyman, this unexpected task has given me great pleasure; I hope that the readers will find the contents enjoyable, too.

Exeter, St. Mary Arches Church

ST MARTIN'S, CATHEDRAL CLOSE

A SMALL church with a big title: St Martin's, in a corner of Cathedral Close, was dedicated on 5 July 1065, "in honour of Our Lord Jesus Christ and of His Holy Cross and of St Mary the Mother of God and of St Martin the Bishop and of all the Saints of God."

Coats of arms acquired over the centuries indicate that perhaps it was a favoured place for quiet prayer by a number of Bishops of Exeter. These include Edmund Lacy 1420–1455, Peter Courtenay 1478–1487, Jonathan Trelawney 1689–1707, and Offspring Blackall 1708–1716.

When Exeter Corporation petitioned Queen Elizabeth in 1582 to reduce the city churches from 17 to five, they selected St Martin's among the five; but their plan was frustrated by the diocese.

In 1656, however, the Commonwealth Parliament decreed that 13 of the 17 buildings be auctioned, including St Martin's, which realised just £100.

Back in diocesan hands with the Restoration of Charles II, the church was repaired, probably at the expense of Mr Philip Hooper, whose bewigged smiling likeness is captured in a wall memorial, seated at a table piled with books and a skull.

The West Country Studies Library has among its papers a curious press cutting from 1825: "On opening a lead coffin deposited 55 years ago of the remains of the Rev. Mr Heron, rector of St

Martin's, the body was found as perfect as when it was placed in the tomb, the flesh yielding to the touch and recovering its smoothness when the finger was removed; a napkin around the head and a shroud covering the corpse were as white and unimpaired as if they had just come from the draper's shop."

It seems that little St Martin's, like this rector, is a born survivor. The church is now well maintained by the Churches Conservation Trust.

Mr Ralph Price, a former lay vicar choral of Exeter Cathedral, pointed out to me that the sanctuary of St Martin's does not face squarely to the east, as in other churches, but slopes back from the south corner to the north.

This is no building error, he believes, but is a feature seen also in some Continental churches, symbolising the traditional artistic representation of Christ's figure on the Cross, His head never erect, but inclining forward from right to left.

ST STEPHEN'S, HIGH STREET

FOR at least 1,000 years, St Stephen's Church has been standing at Exeter's heart, beside the main thoroughfare passing through from West to East Gates in the walled city.

Now, as in earlier times, it has served as a haven for those who seek a moment's refuge from the busy street, and the inscription around the entrance arch is apt and welcoming: "Come ye yourselves apart and rest awhile."

An ancient crypt unearthed during repairs last century is perhaps part of the original chapel raised in Saxon times.

W. G. Hoskins believed that many of Exeter's little churches were first built privately by the rich and noble as centres of worship for their families and tenants.

St Stephen's is registered in the 1086 Domesday survey, and is said to have been given to William the Conqueror's nephew, William Warelwast, third Bishop of Exeter (1107–1137).

Concern for the deprived in inner cities is not new. In 1654 the Countess of Pembroke gave the parish some land outside the East Gate, so that the annual rent of £10 could help "one destitute child, boy or girl, born or residing in the parish of St Stephen's to be put into an apprenticeship in some honest trade or course of living." The charity was still helping one or two young people in the last century.

The mediaeval peace of the city churches was shattered when Cromwell decreed that only four should remain.

So St Stephen's was sold for £250 in 1658 to Toby Allen, who used the cellar (crypt) as a stable. When the Crown was restored two years later, George Parker, merchant and alderman, gave £500 for the complete restoration of the church; but while repairs were in progress fire totally destroyed the building.

Undaunted, faithful parishioners in 1664 again rebuilt the church and provided a new communion set.

A memorial marked the career of William Jackson, who graduated from a chorister to organist of Exeter Cathedral in 1777 and was "a composer of many anthems." The family had come from Moreleigh, and his grandfather gained a fortune making serge.

A friend paid a fulsome tribute to the musician: "In the science of music an eminent professor, whose genius united elegant expression and pure and original melody with peculiar delicacy of harmonic combination." (Rolling Stones take note!)

While Nazi bombs reduced the surrounding area to rubble, the church stood mainly intact, except that fire caused the bells to crash. Their broken remains were moulded into a new bell.

The church is a centre for many worthy causes, the interior being altered to house exhibitions, coffee mornings, and meetings on current affairs. A modern feature at the east end by artist Bobbie Cox – an altar frontal with wall hangings – blends well with the atmosphere of worship, peace, and permanence.

6

ST PANCRAS, WATERBEER STREET

AN ENCLOSED harbour of peace in the heart of a busy city, St Pancras, the tiny ancient church built of Heavitree stone, gives grace to the modern buildings which surround it in the Exeter Guildhall precinct.

Just how long has this place been set aside for Christian worship? When the structure was repaired last century, there was evidence of a Saxon door.

"It has the plan of a Saxon church and has probably come from the earliest days of Christianity in Exeter," Arthur Mee records in his *Devon*.

There is another theory that a church may have been built there even before the Romans left Exeter around AD 400. Because the pavement of the praetorium, or seat of the Roman governor, was found at the end of nearby Waterbeer Street, Beatrix Cresswell wrote: "If a praetorium built by Roman hands, why not a church of Christian Romans, dedicated to a boy saint venerated from the earliest days of the church."

The story of St Pancras is that in 304, as a boy of 14, he accompanied his mother when she was accused by Emperor Diocletian of being a Christian.

When told that so fine looking a lad should not fall for superstitious beliefs but worship the Emperor, Pancras replied that he would bow to no other God but the Christ his mother worshipped. Diocletian killed him on the spot.

The church's east window, presented a century ago by Bishop Tozer, first Bishop of Zanzibar, gives a clue to another tradition about this site. On either side of the crucified Lord are St Pancras and Crediton's St Boniface, Apostle of the Germans.

The historical silence following the Roman departure is broken by a tradition that Boniface, aged 7, received his earliest education from Saxon Wolphard in an abbey near St Pancras Church; so he may well have worshipped here around 680.

Even the simple Norman font has seen some excitement during its 800-odd years. During a time of neglect, it disappeared from the church and was later found in the yard of a public house.

The church's registers record an event in the summer of 1727 which shook the local population: "Between foure and five of the clocke in the morning all the houses in Exeter did shake with an earthquake that people was shakt in their beds from one side to another; twas all over England but dued little damage."

The one sweet-sounding bell in the turret has a Latin inscription proclaiming: "I may be small, but I am heard over a wide area." The letters RN are those of Exeter bellfounder Robert Norton, who in the reign of Henry VI made some of Devon's loveliest bells.

Often disused and neglected since the 1540s, little St Pancras strangely survived while 28 of the city's ancient churches were demolished over the centuries.

When in 1906 Allhallows Church in Goldsmith Street was closed, St Pancras inherited its fine Jacobean pulpit.

During the blitz it became a refuge for worshippers whose churches were damaged or destroyed.

When it became one of the six churches in the Parish of Central Exeter, Rector Michael Selman said of it: "St Pancras has a new purpose. Open each weekday, it provides an opportunity for peace and quiet for those who come to this part of the city in the course of the daily round."

ST PETROCK'S, HIGH STREET

IS ST Petrock's the oldest church in Exeter? Some with a romantic outlook like to think that the 6th century saint from Cornwall travelled on from founding Buckfast Abbey and set up a mission station here, among the British people who continued to live in the city after the Romans departed.

Early mention of the city churches was made in William I's time, and St Petrock's would have been one of the 29 for which the Provost of Exeter was ordered to pay one penny each to the Crown out of the rates.

A deed of 1191 sealed by Bishop Marshall makes it one of the first of the Exeter churches to be mentioned by name.

The church had an important position, being close by the Carfax, or the place where the four main routes met (North, South, Fore, and High Streets).

Extensive rebuilding and additions were made in the 15th century, when St Petrock's was a small but wealthy parish, being at the commercial heart of Exeter.

So much work was done that the building was re-dedicated by Thomas Chard, last Abbot of Ford, acting on behalf of Hugh Oldham, Bishop of Exeter.

With the Guildhall nearby, Mayors of Exeter have had close connections with St Petrock's over the centuries. An old memorial mentioned William Hurst, five times mayor, who died in 1568.

William Wilford, a wealthy merchant and seven times mayor, whose home was next to the church, made his will there in 1413. A contemporary parishioner, in his will of 1411, ordered that 100 poor persons be given proper clothing, including 50 who should carry torches at his funeral.

A seesaw of changes occurred in Reformation times. In 1547 the rood, or carved image of Jesus, was taken down and the building was "made clene" of other ornaments, pictures of saints being "whytelymed."

Six years later, during Queen Mary's reign, the rood and ornaments were restored, and the Latin service book replaced the new English Prayer Book, which was publicly burned.

With Elizabeth I's coronation, rood and ornaments were again swept away – this time for good. The church became an early library, with books in English available for passers-by to read, including "le Bybel", but the volumes were attached to chains.

A plaque to be seen on the tower outside celebrates the widening of the High Street in 1905, after the removal of the crowded mediaeval housing, which had necessitated clerestory windows and a skylight to relieve the gloom inside.

The six bells, reputed to be the lightest peal in Devon, have been put to good use since the church became a centre to train new ringers.

Feoffees still administer ancient parish charities maintaining and allocating alms houses in the city.

St Petrock's found a new role in the 1990s when part of the building was adapted as a day centre for the homeless. Run by Mr Trevor Gardner and financed by Exeter Christians of all denominations, it has had the full support of Rector Michael Selman.

Mr Ramon Yeo, who opened the centre when he was mayor, has a special claim to St Petrock's, as it was the church of one of his ancestors.

8

ST MARY ARCHES, MARY ARCHES STREET

BUILT around 1100, St Mary Arches is the only Devon church to have retained the distinctive Norman arches from which its dedication is derived.

Preb. Norman Davey, last rector of the church, made contact with the only other known St Mary Arches Church – in Austria.

The Exeter church is first named in the will of Peter de Palerna, who in King John's reign left a penny a year to be paid to all of the city's 28 parish churches, which served a population of 2,500 to 3,000 people in mediaeval times.

The church became the favoured centre of worship for merchants, among them the numerous Mayors of Exeter whose memorials were placed in the building. First there was a stone effigy of Thomas Andrew, Mayor in 1505 and 1510.

There is a plaque for Alicia Blackaller, Mayor Andrews' daughter and wife of John Blackaller, who as Mayor during the 1549 Prayer Book Rebellion, kept the city loyal to the King.

John Davy, one of the Davy family of Creedy Park, Sandford, Mayor in 1584, 1594, and 1604, won fame by giving refuge to the King of Portugal when he was driven out by Philip of Spain. The king "was very nobly entertained by the mayor for some considerable time."

Richard Crossing, Mayor in 1654, refused office in 1649 "because the king's government was by violence obstructed."

"A life so good" on the epitaph of Nicholas Brooking (Mayor 1655) refers to his being "one of the few influential persons who remained in the city during one of its most fearful visitations of the plague," historian Beatrix Cresswell writes.

The civic church role ended after more than 300 years with the burial of Burnet Patch, Mayor in 1813.

When John Wesley came to Exeter in November, 1739, Rector Dr Robert Wight offered him the St Mary Arches pulpit for morning and evening services. After morning service, however, Dr Wight cancelled the evening engagement because Wesley's sermon, although sound in doctrine, was "dangerous" and "might lead people into enthusiasm or despair."

The morning after a bombing raid on Exeter in 1942 the Rector, Preb. Edmund Reid, held a communion service for the sisters of St Wilfrid's Community. Later in the day the church was ablaze from spreading fires, and the sisters dashed back to save a processional cross and crucifix.

Mother Lilian (100 in 1997) and the late Sister Elsie, the only surviving members of the community, are fondly remembered by generations of St Wilfrid School old pupils.

The church is home to the colours of Devon's Home Guard, and the names are listed of some of the few of "Dad's Army" in Britain who lost their lives in action, when exchanging fire with a Nazi aircraft.

St Mary Arches was Diocesan Education Centre from 1982, when it became part of the united Central Exeter Parish. Its future is uncertain since the decision to close the centre.

ST OLAVE'S, FORE STREET

ON RECORD as a centre of worship for nearly 1,000 years, St Olave's in Exeter's Fore Street was probably founded as a house chapel for Gytha, Countess of Wessex, mother of England's last Anglo-Saxon ruler, King Harold, who was killed by that stray arrow in the Battle of Hastings.

The only part of what may have been the original church, a small square tower, is visible from the street and is included in the structure of the present larger building.

Tradition claims that a priest of St Olave's helped Countess Gytha to escape to the Continent in 1068, when William the Conqueror began his siege of Exeter.

There is debate about why the church was dedicated to St Olave. For Olave read Olaf, King and patron saint of Norway, who after he was baptised in Rouen, set about converting his countrymen by armed force and died in a fiord battle in 1030.

Among others, he fought Canute, King of Denmark and England, who was related by marriage to Countess Gytha. Why should Gytha dedicate her chapel to a former enemy? Exeter-born historian, Baring-Gould, discusses this, and the theory that a Danish colony settled in the parishes of St Olave and St Edmund (by the river) at that time.

He writes: "It is hard to see that a Danish lady should have felt any enthusiasm for St Olaf, who was bitterly opposed by the Danes."

Whatever the reason, St Olaf is featured in a modern window, and his exploits are romantically recorded in Longfellow's Saga of King Olaf.

After Exeter's capture, William I gave the parish's income to his foundation, Battle Abbey in Sussex.

As years passed, rich merchants built fine homes in the centre of Exeter, then one of England's greatest cities, and among the city parishes, St Olave's prospered. There are memorials to members of the Acland family who worshipped here.

From the middle 1600s, however, richer people moved away from the centre, and their homes were occupied by numerous poorer families.

In Cromwell's time, St Olave's was closed and neglected for a time, but unexpectedly came to life again with the arrival of Protestants fleeing persecution in France in 1685. Four French pastors were allowed to take services for their Huguenot flock in the church for 70 years. The last pastor, Jean Courtail, died on 24 October 1759.

The Bishop of Exeter's survey of 1744 records that St Olave's also served as a charity school for 40 girls and for "30 children of the city to be taught to read the Protestant English Bible."

Last century's greatest expert on bells, the Rev. H. T. Ellacombe, of Clyst St George, described St Olave's one mediaeval bell as "perfect and beautiful." Its Latin inscription echoes this claim: "By my lively voice, I dispel all that is harmful."

But the muffled bell tolled all too often in 1832, when cholera carried off many of the parish's crowded population, living as they did with little sanitation.

After a spell as a chapel for regiments stationed in Exeter, the church last century reverted to a local centre of worship as part of the High Church movement.

With the Rev. Michael Selman as rector, it is one of the churches of the Parish of Central Exeter established in 1971.

MINT METHODIST CHURCH, FORE STREET

AN ANTIQUE table standing inconspicuously near the entrance of Exeter's Mint Methodist Church has a discreet notice: "Not to be used." Behind this modest request is the story of how Methodism first came to Exeter.

John Wesley, as an Anglican clergyman, was already rousing England with his preaching when he spoke at St Mary Arches Church on Sunday morning, 25 November 1739. He was also booked to preach in the evening, but the vicar stopped him, saying: "All you said is true, but it is not guarded. It may lead people into enthusiasm or despair." So the table was produced for the evening rally when Wesley stood on it to preach out of doors. Perhaps it was useful again in 1743, when he spoke to a "vast assembly" in the Castle yard, and for fellow evangelist, George Whitfield, who addressed "upwards of 10,000" in Southernhay Green. Methodism was established, sometimes angering Anglican and old-established Nonconformist churches.

A great opportunity came in 1812. On a site off Mint Lane a large Unitarian Chapel was sold to the Musgrave Alley Chapel Methodists, who then built there a fine Georgian-style church to house 1,000 in 1813. The church flourished. A national ecclesiastical census on 30 March 1851 recorded 550 at morning service, 800 in the evening, and 200 in Sunday School.

A drawback was that the one entrance from the obscure Mint Lane – the iron gate is still there – was often deliberately blocked with carts and rubbish by the hostile owners of the Oatsheaf public house, which then occupied the present frontage on Fore Street. Virtue eventually prevailed when a devout church member, Mr Thomas Rowe, in 1878 bought the freehold of the Oatsheaf inn (which it is unlikely he ever entered). When the lease finally expired, his will enabled the church to demolish the pub and establish Fore Street as its main entrance.

Not that the total abstinence lobby had everything its own way when it was first suggested only unfermented grape juice should be used for Holy Communion. A delay was agreed in deference to one of the trustees, Benjamin Faville Carr, who was a city wine merchant.

Mr Harold Bayley recalled the closure of the Mint School in 1938. Founded in 1848, when there was no general elementary education, it had a roll of nearly 500, but closed for lack of local authority support. Minutes of the last managers' meeting said the school was "strangled by red tape."

There was a crisis in 1965. The old building – similar in style to a Wren London church and praised by John Betjeman in a 1960 visit – was declared unsafe and had to be demolished. Should it be replaced? This was finally decided when the Minister, Peter Bolt, met a Rank Organisation official by chance on an intercity train. "You raise what you can. We will do the rest," the Rank man promised. Meanwhile morning worship continued in the Mint's church hall, and in the evenings in St Mary Major, the Anglican church now itself demolished, which used to stand in front of the Cathedral. A steward, Mr Lawrence Coles, led the symbolic march from the Mint to St Mary Major for the first away evening service.

The fine modern building was opened in 1970, and members celebrated its coming of age by raising £8,000 for a Methodist High School in Zambia, whose chaplain, Graham Shaw, was sponsored for the ministry by the Mint Church.

As for the original "mint", was it one that made coins for Alfred the Great, or another in William I's reign? Nobody seems to know.

ST NICHOLAS PRIORY, THE MINT

WHEN monks from Battle Abbey, Sussex, were directed by William the Conqueror to serve St Olave's Church, nearby they founded in 1089 St Nicholas Priory, part of which has survived to this day in a quiet corner of Exeter.

The priory quickly grew, but when Osbern Fitzosbern (Bishop of Exeter 1072–1103) tried to stop the monks from overzealous bell-ringing, the Norman Archbishop Anselm objected. A subsequent letter by Osbern, written in Anglo-Saxon and preserved in the Cathedral Library, granted the monks leave to ring their bells except at Christmas and Easter Eves and on St Peter's Day, and they were instructed to join the Cathedral canons for Christmas and Palm Sunday processions.

King John, who favoured the Benedictine order, extended the revenues of the priory with the right to hold fairs, but a dispute arose with the municipal authorities, who wanted a larger share of such income.

In 1400 there was consternation when the priory seal was stolen, and the monks feared the thieves might forge deeds conveying away their property, but Bishop Stafford frustrated any such design by ordering an amended seal to be made immediately.

At the priory's dissolution in 1536, dramatic scenes ensued as a workman was directed by the King's representatives to pull down the image of Christ from above the screen.

John Hooker, Chamberlain of Exeter 1555–1601, who was 10 at the time, recorded that certain women – Jone Reve, Elizabeth Glandfield, Agnes Collaton, Alys Mylle, and Jone Rede armed with spikes, shovels, pikes, and "any such tools as they could get" broke down the door and hurled stones.

The terrified workman leaped out of a window. The Mayor restored order, putting the women in jail, but when the task was completed to their satisfaction, the King's men left, asking that the women should be released.

In 1791 Roman Catholics used what remained of the buildings to hold Masses until Sacred Heart Church was built in South Street.

Exeter Corporation bought the priory in 1913. It has since been carefully restored and opened to the public.

ST THOMAS, COWICK STREET

THE BRIDGE now linking Exeter and St Thomas is about a quarter of the length of the mediaeval stone bridge of 700 feet and 18 arches, on which in 1249 a woman hermit made her home, sometimes delaying the traffic. The city fathers were most patient, or were they perhaps afraid of disturbing a holy person? Imagine the wail of sirens if such a vigil were started now!

The hermit may have found refuge later in a church built at the St Thomas end of the bridge about 1257. The first vicar, "Henry" was instituted by Bishop Walter Bronescombe in 1261, but the river caused constant flooding and finally the building was washed out to sea.

Parishioners asked the Prior of Cowick Monastery (a small establishment of about four monks) to build another church on safer ground. It was consecrated by Bishop Stafford in 1412.

Like ten other Devon churches, it kept its dedication to St Thomas Becket, despite Henry VIII's attempt to suppress all such dedications honouring the "turbulent priest" who had defied his ancestor, Henry II, and was martyred in Canterbury Cathedral.

With the 1549 Prayer Book Rebellion, however, St Thomas found its own turbulent priest in Vicar Robert Welsh (1536–49), who joined the Catholic rebels laying siege to Exeter from St Thomas in the west and St Sidwell's in the east.

A strong wrestler and good shot with long and cross bows, Welsh yet persuaded the rebel leaders not to burn the city, because many citizens, including the mayor, preferred the Latin Mass; but he made a tactical error in hanging, on Exe Island, a messenger captured en route to the King's Army. After the rebels' defeat at Clyst St Mary by Lord Russell, and his German and Italian mercenaries, Welsh was hanged in Catholic vestments from the church tower. It is ironic that his death should have been engineered by Continental troops. In these days of European integration is it an omen for the future?

After this, by no coincidence, the church was no longer dedicated to Thomas Becket, but St Thomas the Apostle.

The infamous tower crashed to the ground when the church was destroyed by fire in 1645 and the present building erected in its place.

Inside, the fine 15th century eagle lectern differs from similar "birds" in Ottery St Mary and Salcombe Regis because "feathers" were carved on it at a later date. This lectern was secured from Exeter Cathedral by another vicar, John Medley (1838–45), whose later work as the missionary Bishop of Fredericton earned him the post of Archbishop of Canada from 1879 to 1892. While at St Thomas he was "an unfailing friend of the poor."

A memorial to his first wife, Christina, who died 1842, was carved by her father, John Bacon, a renowned sculptor, and has been described as "great Christian art."

The church's strong Canadian connection is also kept alive through a second missionary, John Horden, a Sunday School teacher at St Thomas, who became Bishop of Moosonoe from 1872 until his death at Fort Moose in 1893.

Grandfathers of three historic figures Sir Joshua Reynolds, General George Monk (Duke of Albemarle), and General Gordon are all buried at St Thomas. Gordon was about to enter the church to see his grandfather's memorial when summoned by a telegram to go to Khartoum – and his death.

In 1985 the Rev. Alan White became Team Rector of the St Thomas parish, which has four churches and 16,000 parishioners.

ST MICHAEL'S, ALPHINGTON

A GUARDED welcome is given visitors to St Michael and All Angels, Alphington, by a 1720 notice above the entrance, asking that they "remove their pattens", lest the noise disturb the congregation.

It hardly applies today, unless stiletto heels make a fashion comeback, because the "patten" is no longer needed as a type of clog or metal frame to lift shoes above the muddy lanes.

Another use for footwear is revealed in a mediaeval panel picture on the north aisle screen. It shows the "blessed" Sir John Schorne, rector of Long Marston (Bucks), once venerated as a local saint, proudly holding a boot in which he had somehow imprisoned the Devil. Sir John is also remembered for his "feat" in St George's Chapel, Windsor – but nowhere else.

In a neighbouring panel, painted by "The Master of Alphington", St Dunstan, patron saint of blacksmiths, demonstrates a different mode of restraining Satan – by holding his nose with a pair of red-hot tongs.

The present church of about 1480 was built on the site of an earlier building, of which the font remains. Made of Beer stone around 1,000 years ago, it is either Saxon or early Norman.

Like all old parishes, Alphington has its share of notable rectors.

William Oldreive, appointed 1536, survived the execution of his famous patron, Henry Courtenay, Marquis of Exeter, during the beheading times of Henry VIII. (The Marquis' son, Edward, was created the first Earl of Devon by Queen Mary in 1553.)

Unlike his unfortunate neighbour who was hanged from the tower of St Thomas Church, Oldreive avoided involvement in the Prayer Book Rebellion, and kept his head down during the changes under Edward VI, Mary, and Elizabeth I.

By his will, made in 1558 and proved in 1589, he was buried in the church and left forty shillings for its upkeep. Four poor women were left 5d each for holding tapers at his burial, and his stock of firewood was divided among the needy.

Parliament troops used the church as a stable in 1644 during the Civil War.

William Ellicombe, rector 1780–1831, has a memorial window; another shows his daughter teaching the village children on the Rectory lawn; and a third commemorates his son, John, killed in Holland during the Napoleonic Wars.

To the left of the churchyard path, cobbled in 1844, is a memorial to a boy, George Coles, killed by lightning during a storm in 1826 which also badly damaged the tower.

Severe damage was also caused by a malicious fire in October, 1986, but Rector Mark Bate and his congregation met the challenge to raise the £60,000 needed over and above the £365,000 insurance payment to restore vestry, loft, roof, vestments, and provide a new organ.

Mr Bate was amused that the name of one of the previous rectors was shared by the former Prime Minister. "You could say that I am John Major's successor," he said.

A large, active congregation responds each Sunday to the call of the "eight musical bells" dedicated by a Bishop of Exeter 250 years ago.

ST MICHAEL'S, DINHAM ROAD

ST MICHAEL'S, Mount Dinham, built in 1868, has the tallest spire (230 feet) of any church west of Salisbury – a landmark to match the Cathedral towers.

Although St Michael's has always had a high church tradition, it was an evangelical John Dinham, city silversmith and tea merchant, who first conceived the idea to build a chapel on the site last century. The growth of prostitution among young girls in Exeter alarmed Dinham, and when it was proposed to sell the factory site, now occupied by the church, for a fairground, he thought it would be a breeding ground for more vice. With help, he bought the land and built almhouses "for the deserving poor," and planned a school and chapel there to serve the impoverished community.

When Dinham died in 1864, the cause was taken up by merchant William Gibbs, member of another old Devon family who occupied Pytte House, Clyst St George, from the 16th century. At a cost of £21,000, Gibbs built a grand neo-Gothic church, suitable for Anglo-Catholic worship. He also built St David's Church School for £1,100 and endowed a priest's salary with £2,095.

Originally designed to serve a poor district, it was fitting that the missionary Bishop of Fredericton, later first Archbishop of Canada, Dr John Medley, should consecrate the new church in the absence of Bishop Phillpotts of Exeter. When Vicar of St Thomas, Exeter, from 1838 to 1845, Dr Medley was known as "the familiar friend of the poor". With its "most modern" gas-lighting, however, the new church attracted the wealthy from other parts of the city, including the mother church of St David's. This eventually persuaded loyal St David's people to replace their own church with a more splendid building in 1900.

But while it was being built, for three years the two congregations were drawn together for worship at St Michael's. A non-stipendiary priest serving St Michael's, the Rev. Peter Lee, said that for many years after opening, men and women sat on different sides of the church. "The reason could have been nothing to do with tradition, but rather to keep young people under control during evening service when the church was dark."

During the Second World War the complete blackout at St Michael's made it one of the few city venues suitable for concerts, including performances by Isobel Bailey and Roy Henderson.

Fr W. W. Waller, fondly remembered priest 1945–58, had served in the war as an interpreter for Japanese POWs.

He and Bishop Wilfrid Westall, Monsignor Tobin (RC of Sacred Heart Church), and Fr Frank Rice (Vicar of David's) took turns to host dinners monthly, with Leonard Dingle, a member of St Michael's and a teacher, always acting as chef.

The Rev. John Henton, Vicar of both St David's and St Michael's from 1991, supported the church institute which drew wide interest with a series of topical debates.

ST MARY STEPS, WEST STREET

THE THREE figures above the clock on the church tower of St Mary Steps, Exeter, have long fascinated people of all ages.

As the clock strikes the hour, the stout man in the centre nods his head, and the two beside him sound the quarter hours with long hammers at their feet.

Who were they meant to represent? Some have seen a likeness to Henry VIII in the seated man wearing breastplate and helmet, with two soldiers carrying pikes to guard him.

Local tradition tells a different tale. Long ago, when there was no public clock, Matthew the Miller, whose mill was nearby, was a model of punctuality. Residents who had timepieces would set them as they heard his cart pass their doors, always at the same hour, both morning and evening.

After he died, the story goes, the church clock was erected – the actual date was 1619 – as a memorial to him and so that the parishioners would continue to know the hour.

The figures and the clock itself have been known to this day as Matthew the Miller and his sons. Old maps show the mill leat passing near the church outside the city wall.

A church occupied the present site, just inside the West Gate of the city, since at least 1150, its name being derived from Stepcote Hill, which was then the main route from the West into the centre of Exeter. The present building rose in the 15th century but incorporated the earlier Norman "tub" font.

Preb. Michael Moreton, rector of St Mary Steps from 1959 until recently, writes that the earliest fonts were the "bath" type for total immersion of adults; the more recent are pedestals with a basin, suitable for infants held in arms.

St. Mary's Steps Church, Exeter.

"The tub font, typical of the intervening centuries, is a witness to the occasional surviving practice of baptism of adults by partial immersion," he explains.

The first named rector, mentioned in Bishop Bronescombe's register, was Alan de Baucumbe, instituted 1273, but there were probably earlier rectors.

In those times the congregation stood for services, but when sermons became fashionable from the 15th century, the building was enlarged with a south aisle to allow for seats.

When a bishop's census was made of Exeter Diocese in 1744, it was reported that communion services were held monthly, alternating with nearby St Edmund's-by-the-Bridge, with between 100 and 140 communicants.

The rector had a prejudice, as he reported: "I have by best calculation 200 families, and no more than four whole families of Dissenters of any kinds." The people were mostly poor, living in cramped conditions in the available houses.

The church interior, restored over the centuries, contains work by Harry Hems, famous craftsman in wood and stone, in 1866, and a beautiful modern east window by John Hayward (1966).

The last three rectors, Henry Burdett, Augustus Browne and Michael Moreton, served over a span of 100 years.

ST DAVID'S, HELE ROAD

BECAUSE St David's, Exeter, is one of only three Devon churches dedicated to the Welsh saint (the others are at Ashprington and Thelbridge), it has been speculated that the great missionary once visited the city and founded a chapel outside its walls in the 7th century.

Communications between Wales and "West Wales", as Devon and Cornwall were once called, were close in those early times before Athelstan, King Alfred's grandson, drove the Celts out of Exeter in process of making England one kingdom for the first time in the 10th century.

The inscription on the foundation stone of the present St David's building, laid by Mrs Thornton West on 28 July, 1897, records that it was "in the 1300th year of the mission of St Augustine to the English, in honour of St David who about that time was maintaining the light of the Gospel among the Britons, and the 60th year of the reign of Queen Victoria, under whom all nations in the Empire enjoy light and unity."

In days when Victorian architecture (and values) were under siege, the church received high praise from that master of good taste, Sir John Betjeman, in a radio talk on "A hundred years of architecture in Wessex." He gave first place to St David's, Exeter, as an example of Victorian architecture.

Besides being a fine centre for worship, W. D. Caroe's design in grey Bath stone created a splendid setting for the many musical events for which it is the venue.

It replaced another big building with accommodation for 600 worshippers which stood on the same site from 1816 to 1897, called the Pepper-Box Church because of its unusual tower.

Outside the ancient walls of Exeter, St David's Hill and the area to the north were part of the manor of Duryard where after the Norman Conquest in 1066 Norman kings on visits to the city would hunt deer and boar in the woodlands.

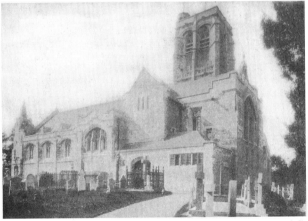

Celtic families remained in the area, and historian Joyce Greenaway records that, to this day, the lower St David's Hill is called "Little Britain".

In those early days the chapel was under the control of the Vicars of Heavitree, who appointed curates to care for the churches outside the city walls at St David's and St Sidwell's.

It was during the troubled times of 1541 that a new church was built. Six years later the churchwardens found they had to sell a chalice for £3.16s to buy a new English Bible (translated by Bishop Miles Coverdale of Exeter) and an English communion book. The chalice weighed 16 ounces and was sold at the going rate of silver in the city – 5 shillings an ounce.

St David's open meadow was a favourite picnic ground for Exeter citizens in summer.

The three-day Lammas Fair included a market where bread, wine and ale were traded. When Charles II became King in 1660, city people rejoiced with a bonfire on St David's Hill, and "wine flowed, even on the road." In 1816 people celebrated their new church opening at the Barnstaple Inn and "gave a loaf of bread and a quart of beer to 300 poor."

Its magnificent reredos holding attention from the moment of entry, St David's is a church of which Exeter can be proud. John Henton, Vicar since 1991, drew support from many sources within the parish, including the church school and Exeter College.

The church has been kept open with stewards in the middle of the day, giving city workers and students an opportunity for quiet reflection.

SOUTH STREET BAPTIST CHURCH

THE DINING room of the Cathedral Deanery was the first recorded meeting place for Baptists in Exeter, but Dean William Peterson was not there. He had been ejected from home and Cathedral with the arrival of Cromwell's men and was living frugally with his wife in a Stoke Canon cottage by selling what furniture they had rescued from the Deanery.

Meanwhile, John Carew, one of the judges at Charles I's trial, bought the Deanery from the city council, and Baptist meetings were convened there by the minister, Capt Paul Hobson, a member of Cromwell's Army.

By 1656 an Act of Parliament ordered that "the best Exeter church available" should be placed at the disposal of the Baptist congregation. This was probably St Paul's in Paul Street, which was eventually demolished in 1936.

When Charles II became King in 1660, Mr Peterson returned to his Deanery, but the Baptists, along with other Dissenters, met secretly for 12 years until the Declaration of Indulgence (1672) gave them a measure of freedom. Persecution returned, however, with the failure of the Duke of Monmouth's rebellion against James II in 1685. Miss Maureen Sleeman, church secretary and President of the Devon and Cornwall Baptist Association, recorded that Col Abraham Holmes, thought to be the Exeter Baptist minister, was one of a party of rebels executed at the Cobb in Lyme Regis. The story goes that the party had to march to their death because the horses refused to pull the sledges containing the prisoners.

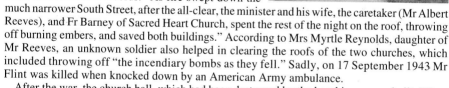

More freedom came with King William in 1689, and the Baptists held meetings in Catherine Street and Candy's Lane until Benjamin Heath, a church member and "influential merchant in the city", bought the South Street site, and a chapel was erected in 1725. An oil portrait of Mr Heath's son, who became Town Clerk, is in the Guildhall.

The present building was erected in 1825, and over the years it has acted as a centre in founding and ministering to village churches in the Exeter district. A group of 30 members in 1933 founded Exeter's Pinhoe Road Baptist Church.

Minister at the time of the Blitz was the Rev. Matthew Flint. Miss Sleeman records: "As fire swept down the much narrower South Street, after the all-clear, the minister and his wife, the caretaker (Mr Albert Reeves), and Fr Barney of Sacred Heart Church, spent the rest of the night on the roof, throwing off burning embers, and saved both buildings." According to Mrs Myrtle Reynolds, daughter of Mr Reeves, an unknown soldier also helped in clearing the roofs of the two churches, which included throwing off "the incendiary bombs as they fell." Sadly, on 17 September 1943 Mr Flint was killed when knocked down by an American Army ambulance.

After the war, the church hall, which had been destroyed by the bombing, was rebuilt. When it was decided, however, to buy the Kennaways Wine Store alongside the church, the hall was sold to the Shilhay Community, and the present Palace Gate Centre, created out of the former wine premises, was opened by Sir Peter Mills MP, chairman of the House of Commons Christian Fellowship, on 2 June 1979.

The Rev. John Stroud, a recent minister, found that the centre built a community spirit for many living in the city. People of all kinds and ages find help and companionship through the numerous groups with headquarters at Palace Gate.

The latest joint venture with the Parish of Central Exeter is the Church Urban Fund project employing Mr Trevor Gardner as a community development officer to work among homeless, lonely and distressed people.

The church has exchange links with a congregation in Bad Homburg.

The close liaison of all city centre churches is proof that the denominations have come some way towards reunion since the far-off times when the Exeter Baptists met at the Deanery.

SACRED HEART, SOUTH STREET

WHILE most of the buildings in South Street were destroyed during the Exeter blitz 50 years ago, two standing side by side were spared – the Roman Catholic Church of the Sacred Heart and South Street Baptist Church. Was it a miracle – a little God-pocket of preservation? That may be, but it seems God had some help in the person of the Sacred Heart parish priest, the Rev. Fr Thomas Barney, who was spied during the raid standing of the flat roof of the Presbytery between the two churches, sweeping off the incendiaries as they fell. As he performed the brave deed, it is tempting to conjecture that the priest was humming one of the hit songs of the time, 'Praise the Lord and Pass the Ammunition'.

In any case, the church, now more than 100 years old, remains as the city's centre of Catholic worship. Its smaller predecessor was founded in 1791 in the remains of St Nicholas Priory, behind the Mint Methodist Church. The year 1791 is a landmark, because Roman Catholics were then given freedom of worship in England for the first time since Queen Elizabeth I's reign.

A notable priest at the Mint Chapel was Fr George Oliver, author of Catholic history, especially in the West Country, who became a historic figure himself during the Exeter cholera epidemic of 1832. Exeter was then a city of narrow streets without sewers and the Exe was so polluted that fish floated dead on its surface. Church bells tolled the deaths of 440 before the plague ran its course. George Oliver remained at his post the whole time attending sick and dying, and afterwards was presented with a silver salver and altar cruets from grateful citizens.

Meanwhile Sacred Heart history records say that Henry Phillpotts, Bishop of Exeter and father of 18 children, left the city during the epidemic, returning only to conduct a service of thanksgiving in the Cathedral when it ended. Phillpotts was no friend of Roman Catholicism, having opposed the Emancipation Bill of 1829, which gave Catholics full civil rights after nearly 300 years. Later his own chaplain, William Maskell, joined the Roman Catholic Church just before the Catholic Diocese of Plymouth was founded in 1851 to cover Devon, Cornwall, and Dorset.

The growing congregation moved to the new church in South Street when it was blessed by Bishop Clifford of Clifton on 18 November 1884. It was built on the site of the Bear Inn, which in the Middle Ages was the town house of the Abbots of Tavistock, and no doubt a rival to the ancient White Hart across the street.

Among the many dedicated Sacred Heart priests who have served both church and community was Canon George Hobson, chairman of the Hospital Board at the time of the opening of the Heavitree Hospital. More recently, Canon Keith Balmont (parish priest 1967–88) ministered with great sensitivity during a time of change, including the switch from the Latin Mass to English. He was assistant priest before the war, in which he served as a chaplain, and helped after retirement until his death. Parish priest from 1990, Fr Doyle was assistant priest 1970–75.

There are close links with other denominations in the city centre, including Exeter Cathedral, where the first Roman Catholic Mass since the Reformation was celebrated on 16 April 1976. Fr Harry Doyle recalled with pleasure being one of the 28 priest concelebrants with Canon Balment at the service, attended by 2,000 people from the Exeter Deanery.

Thanks to a successful appeal in the 1980s to replace the roof, the spacious church building is in good shape.

SALVATION ARMY TEMPLE, FRIAR,S WALK

UNIVERSAL respect and affection for the Salvation Army came after early battles, some of them violent, even in the streets of Exeter

Founded by General William Booth, a Methodist minister, the movement came to Exeter when Corps 142 was formed in 1881.

Exeter Temple, built in 1833 near Friars Gate, the site where Franciscans made their headquarters 600 years earlier, was originally a Quaker Hall, later sold to the Temperance Society, and finally bought by General Booth in 1882.

After initial success – 1,000 people were unable to gain seats in the temple which held 700 – corps members were attacked, both indoors and outdoors, by a "Skeleton Army" led by a "Captain" Figgy Martin, with a banner inscribed: "Death to the Salvationists."

Violence reached such a pitch that on 11 March 1882 Exeter's Mayor issued a proclamation: "Whereas several breaches of the peace and riotous collisions have lately been occasioned by processions of persons calling themselves the 'Salvation Army' and 'Skeleton Army' through the public streets of Exeter ... causing terror and annoyance to the citizens ... notice is hereby given that such processions cannot be permitted to take place..."

Corps leader Capt John Trenhail was put on trial for singing hymns in the street, but was acquitted with a caution.

But Devonian Lord Coleridge, of Ottery St Mary, Lord Chief Justice, came down firmly on the side of the Salvationists, ruling that their processions and singing were "absolutely lawful."

The troubles subsided by 1886, and the corps was free to fight the ills of drunkenness and poverty over the years. So popular was the cause that in 1889 the Temple was extended to hold 2,000 and given an imposing new front.

By 1904 civic approval was finally given in the words of the Mayor and celebrated artist, F. J. Widgery: "All decent and good citizens welcome the Army as an agent for the common good of the land."

By then the corps was providing 200 children with daily breakfasts of cocoa and buns and gave those with bare feet vouchers to buy shoes at a city shop.

Under Sidney Cox, bandmaster for 56 years, the band's reputation grew, playing at the prison, hospitals, civic occasions, and at Exeter Cathedral in 1925 while the organ was being repaired.

In her centennial history (1981) Mrs Maurice Hawker chose this item from the corps archives: "On Christmas Eve 1915 the band played to 3 a.m...."

In the 1920s the big hall was packed for meetings, and the officers apologised to the many who could not find seats.

One item from the 75th anniversary book typifies how Exeter's life has been spiritually enriched over the years.

"During the command of 'Angel Adjutant' Kate Lee, the worst man in the city got converted and became quiet as a lamb. As a result, the Chief Constable is reputed to have said he could manage with six less constables on a Saturday night."

ST LEONARD'S, TOPSHAM ROAD

SLIM, elegant, and looking strangely frail as it is approached up Topsham Road, the 145-foot spire of St Leonard's Church, Exeter, is yet securely based, according to a newspaper report of 1886: "The foundations of the spire are carried down below the level of the river road and rest on a bed of concrete."

In 1903 Westley Bothamley, the only rector to climb to the top of the spire, inspected its condition, and was praised by parishioners for saving them a big sum of money.

The first St Leonard's was built about 1100 on the hill outside the city walls by Richard de Redvers, first Earl of Devon. The land was part of his Exminster Manor estate. He also built a priory by the River Exe, just below.

One of the early rectors, Lucas, earned notoriety on suspicion of being among clergy who plotted the death of a Cathedral precentor, but Exeter's mayor was hanged for the murder on 26 December 1285.

Two women hermits found refuge in the churchyard hut beside Parker's Well, a spring thought to have healing powers. The first, Alice, who had the bishop's leave to settle there in 1397, was succeeded 50 years later by Christine Holby, who said she had been driven from Kildare Convent by "wild Irish".

People paid dawn visits to the well hoping to cure eye ailments up to the last century. A local lad who became Chief Justice took the title Baron Gifford of Parker's Well.

Parishioner George Plimsole also made a name for himself when he stopped huntsmen entering the church in pursuit of a fox, which he later secretly released.

The Baring family, founders of Exeter Bank and later the famous London merchant bank, used great wealth gained in the wool trade to buy most of the parish land in the 18th century and became patrons of the church.

As noisy traffic increased up Topsham Road, John Baring had it diverted in 1779 down the familiar dip beside the church, and built a bridge overhead, from what is now Barnardo Road, so that the family could reach the church in peace.

A new church erected in 1833 proved unsatisfactory, and the present building, designed by R. M. Fulford, rose 40 years later. A member of the Baring family, the Earl of Northbrook, laid the foundation stone to celebrate his safe return from serving as Viceroy of India.

The Royal West of England School for the Deaf, built beside St Leonard's in 1828, proved helpful as a venue for Sunday worship when the church was twice damaged by arson in 1990.

Services resumed in 1993 in the refurbished building, which now has cushioned pews, and the parish earned its status as one of the most spiritually alive in the south-west.

Apart from traditional overseas missionary commitments, under the leadership of Rector John Skinner £250,000 was raised by local people in 1992 for a new church centre.

SOUTHERNHAY UNITED REFORMED CHURCH

AT FIRST glance Southernhay seems too modern a building to occupy such a favoured site at ancient Exeter's heart. A closer look at the tower and spire, however, gives a clue that they were built some time ago – 122 years in fact, as part of the 1,000-seat Congregationalist church built there in 1870.

Congregationalists emerged in Devon as some of their number joined the Pilgrim Fathers who sailed from Plymouth in 1620. The county leader, Lewis Stucley, son of Sir John Stucley, Bt of Afton between Chulmleigh and Witheridge, and a chaplain to Oliver Cromwell, first preached in Exeter Cathedral in 1650 by permission of the Exeter City Council. He persuaded the council, which had taken control of all church property and expelled the bishop and dean, to divide the Cathedral with a wall separating choir and nave. The Congregationalists worshipped in the nave; the Presbyterians, for the time being the official English Church, used the choir; and the Baptists met in the Deanery. With the return of bishop and dean in 1660, the wall was removed and the Nonconformist churches went underground. Stucley stayed in Exeter and as restrictions eased in 1672, he led worship for about 150 in the home of Nicholas Savery, a linen draper of St Petrock's parish.

The first Congregationalist meeting house was built in Castle Lane in 1689, with John Ashwood as leader. A man who had narrowly missed execution for his part in the Monmouth Rebellion, he drew strong local support. By 1715 there were 400 covenanted members.

In 1796 members bought the old county gaol in Castle Street, "then a sink of filth, pestilence, and profligation", and built a new meeting house on the site which opened in 1797. The building is now the Royal British Legion headquarters.

The flock built a new church for £9,000 in Southernhay in 1870 with room for 1,000 worshippers. The Gothic decorated style was unique for local Free Churches at that time.

Sunday School figures issued in 1871 record 220 boy pupils (average attendance 140) and 336 girls (average 290), with 34 teachers in all. Electric light was introduced in 1899.

Fire bombs which destroyed the building on 4 May, 1942, could not have come at a worse time, because there was an interregnum and no new minister had been appointed. The Southernhay Methodist Church offered a temporary home. In his

history, Allan Brockett recorded how members met under the Rev. Phillip Rogers, of Plymouth, and announced: "Though our house is destroyed, we declare our resolve to maintain the home, that family life whose ties are more real... now that the props are gone."

In 1946 the Congregationalists bought the other Southernhay church from the Methodists – for a temporary home.

In 1957 the present church was built beside the tower, which had survived the bombs, at a cost of £65,000.

The organ of the old Southernhay Methodist Church, demolished in 1962, was transferred to the new building and has since been rebuilt into an outstanding instrument used in Exeter Festival recitals. The pulpit and choir stalls were gifts from American Congregational Churches, and one of the stained glass windows depicts the *Mayflower* which transported the Pilgrim Fathers.

In 1972 the church became part of the national union with the Presbyterians to form the United Reformed Church.

ST SIDWELL'S, SIDWELL STREET

EXETER'S own saint, the maiden Sidwella, daughter of a Celtic nobleman, Benna, was murdered by pagan Saxon reapers with their scythes outside the east wall of the city, maybe in AD 740. A church was built over the place, which became a shrine for pilgrims from near and far over succeeding centuries to honour her memory. In recent times a mould for making pilgrims' souvenirs was found in the city High Street. So great was her reputation, that the 14th-century east window in Exeter Cathedral conspicuously portrays St Sidwella, with her symbols – a scythe and a well. Legends say a spring gushed from the ground at her death, and a well on the site did in fact provide water until late last century for the Close at the Cathedral, which held the manor rights east of the city walls.

Successive churches were built on the St Sidwell site until the catastrophic Nazi raids of 1942, when the fourth building was destroyed, along with 800 houses in the suburb, which sustained the greatest share of bomb damage in the city.

A temporary church was replaced with the present St Sidwell's on 23 April 1959. Unpretentious outside, the interior has two outstanding examples of post-war art. At the east end is a mural, Christ in Glory, by Hens Feibusch, a Jewish refugee from the Nazis, who later became a Christian. The big stained glass window in the east end, combining St Sidwell's martyrdom and the Nazi bombing of Exeter, is the work of James Paterson, of Bideford.

The story in between, from the 8th to 20th century, has not been without excitement. In the 13th century, the Mayor and the Dean and Chapter were involved in unseemly disputes about the boundary line between St Sidwell's and the city. The church was seized by the forces of the Prayer Book Rebellion in 1549, while Exeter was under siege, and Sir Walter Raleigh's father (also Walter), who supported the new English prayer book, was held as a prisoner there.

Cavaliers were also imprisoned in the church in 1646, when the city was captured by Roundheads, and a leading citizen, Mr Hugh Grove, was later executed at Exeter Castle for plotting against the Commonwealth and buried at St Sidwell's.

A happier event was the foundation in 1665 of St Sidwell's Church School by the Dean and Chapter. It is still thriving, with 300 pupils, a harmonious centre of learning for children of different ethnic backgrounds.

The Rev. Sabine Baring-Gould, Devon historian, born and baptised in St Sidwell's parish in 1834, thought St Sidwell lived in the 6th century, and that her brother became the famous St Paul of Leon in France.

Rector Francis Courtenay was at the centre of the Surplice Riots of 1849. The wearing of the linen garment in the pulpit roused the wrath of Exeter people, and a crowd estimated at 2,000 shouting people pelted the Rector with mud and eggs.

24

HEAVITREE UNITED REFORMED CHURCH

WAYSIDE pulpits on two church notice boards, facing opposite ways, hold the attention of thousands going to and from Exeter city centre each day, with messages long associated with Mr Bob Vanstone.

Although the present imposing building was erected in 1902, the story of the Congregational churches in Exeter goes back to the 17th century, when a chaplain to Cromwell, Lewis Stucley, younger son of Sir John Stucley of West Worlington, gained civic permission to hold services in the nave of Exeter Cathedral.

All this changed when the Anglican deans returned at the Restoration of Charles II, and the Congregationalists built their first chapel in Castle Lane in 1689.

They moved to the new Southernhay church in 1870. About this time Joseph Hayman also opened a room in his house at Stafford Villas, Heavitree (now 83 Fore Street), for worship. The growing flock bought the site known as Homefield House and built a little church in the garden in 1885.

With the help of a wealthy retired minister, the Rev. Harold Row, Homefield House was replaced with the present large church, hall, and several rooms in 1902.

The Rev. Arthur Axe (Minister 1907–1919), used carpentry skills to make the pulpit and other furnishings.

Young people look with awe at a large wooden dish once used in cannibal feasts in Papua New Guinea. It was presented in 1948 by a converted chieftain to Avis Martin, a Heavitree member who served with the London Missionary Society.

An account of how women became involved in the governing body was given by Mrs Betty Ellis. In 1902, women were first permitted to vote at church meetings.

It was 1928, however, before one was elected a deacon (elder), but a few were so outraged that she resigned immediately. Recently six men and five women have served as elders.

One of the great characters of the early days was local barber Arthur Osbourne, who was superintendent of the Sunday School, a member of the choir, and never missed a Sunday's worship even in frail old age after a lifetime of service.

The longest serving minister, the Rev. David Avis (1966–1980), and his wife Joan, contributed much to the church's life.

The old Southernhay Church was destroyed in the blitz of May 1942, and Heavitree was also hit, the Row memorial window being destroyed and the roof losing 3,000 tiles.

Four members have been ordained – the Revs Brian Nuttall, Anthony Tucker, George Ellis, and Ian Knowles.

Sam Honeywill and Don Rattue had leading roles in arranging the first church's centenary celebrations in 1985.

CHURCH OF THE BLESSED SACRAMENT, HEAVITREE

BASED on a design of the historic St Paul Outside-the-Wall Basilica in Rome, the Roman Catholic Church of the Blessed Sacrament, Heavitree, has made a unique contribution to Exeter's architecture.

Pleasing external features include the cherry-red brick contrasting with the white stone chequered corners, window surrounds, and ornamental roof parapet. The semicircular apse housing the sanctuary at the east end is gracefully guarded by ten white pillars of classical design.

There was quite a stir in Exeter when the big new church, built by the firm of Mr E. B. Wheatley, was blessed in a public service by the Catholic Bishop of Plymouth, the Rt Rev. J. P. Barratt, on Saturday, 28 May 1932.

For the Latin Mass celebrated by the bishop next morning, admittance was by ticket only because of the great interest of people in Devon and beyond.

Although the faithful had dug deeply to make the money available for such an ambitious project, members of the Robinson family, latterly resident in St Marychurch, Torquay, were major contributors towards this church and others in Chelston (Torquay), Bishopsteignton, and in St Budeaux and Crownhill in Plymouth.

The interior which greeted those first crowded congregations was just as striking as the exterior.

All eyes were at once drawn to the great white arch of the sanctuary, with its baldacchino, or canopy, supported by six marble pillars, covering the altar.

Contrasting coloured marbles and onyx make the setting for the shrine of the Virgin and Child, and the 14 stations of the cross were carved in wood and painted.

The font is composed of marble from Ashburton and Torquay quarries and was made by a Devon craftsman.

First priest of the new church, Fr Tyman, had a remarkable escape during a German air raid. Something prompted him to go over to the church just before a bomb crashed into his presbytery. Other bombs destroyed the original stained glass windows in the church and damaged the tower.

The church serves a wide area to east and south, the nearest Catholic churches (apart from Sacred Heart also in the city) being at Ottery St Mary, Cullompton, and Topsham.

Father Paddy Conlon, at the time of publication, was the one priest serving 600 weekly communicants and was thankful for the growing support received from the trained laity.

ST MICHAEL'S HEAVITREE

ALTHOUGH well outside the walled city of Exeter, Heavitree was for centuries the centre of the Saxon kings' Manor of Wonford. It was thought courts and councils were held by a great tree, growing on the site of the present churchyard, beside the main Roman Road into Exeter (now the High Street).

Did the village get its name from this "Hefa's tree" or *heafod treow* (the chief tree)? Nobody is sure, but Prof. W. G. Hoskins thought it was the oldest Christian site outside Exeter, and a church was probably built before AD 700.

Local historian Hazel Harvey conjectured that the present yew tree in the church grounds may well have grown from the trunk of an original sacred tree, perhaps a meeting centre for the Celtic Kings of Dumnonia long before the Romans or Saxons came to Exeter.

In Anand Chetan and Diana Brueton's book, *The Sacred Yew*, the life-span of some self-rejuvenating yews has been estimated at 5,000 years. Yew trees also marked the sites of Druid worship.

The site has seen much building activity in the last 1,000 years. A 12th-century church was altered in the 14th and again in the 15th century and entirely restored in 1541. The nave was rebuilt 1844–46 and the new tower erected for the Queen's Jubilee in 1887.

Heavitree was the centre for rural parishes outside Exeter, being until the middle of last century "mother" church for St Leonard's, St David's, St Sidwell's, and St Margaret's, Topsham. The recorded list of vicars from 1280 includes one named in a feud between Bishop Quivel and the Dean, sparked by the murder of the Cathedral precentor on 5 November 1283.

The Mayor of Exeter, Alured de Porta, was hanged for the crime on 26 December 1285, but others allegedly involved, including the Vicar of Heavitree, escaped trial through a legal loophole.

Richard Hooker, the great mediating Anglican theologian whose carved figure sits in solitary splendour on the Cathedral Green, was born in Heavitree in 1554.

With the many building alterations, it seems one memorial has been lost which recorded the death of Thomas Spyer on 25 June 1625, at the ripe old age of 106.

There is a remaining memorial stone, however, in memory of Thomas Gorges, of Heavitree, Esqr, and his wife Rose. "Hee departed this life 17th Oct, 1670, and Shee 14th April, 1671," – and this celebrated epitaph:

The loving turtle having lost her mate
Begged shee might enter ere they shut the gate,
Their dust here lies whose soules to Heaven are gonne,
And waite till angels rowle away the stone.

A whiff of Barchester surrounds the alabaster reredos, depicting New Testament scenes, behind the main altar.

It was first erected in Exeter Cathedral in 1874, but Bishop Frederick Temple was told by Archdeacon William Phillpotts, son of the former bishop, that such carved figures were illegal. While a lower court ruled the archdeacon was right, an appeal to the Privy Council gave approval for the reredos to stay.

The late Rev. Donald Madge, long associated with the parish, recalled that when the foundations of the work disintegrated, it was thought unsafe to restore, so was offered to Heavitree and erected in its present position at a cost of £2,000 in 1969.

Heavitree parish, with a population of 22,000, the third largest in Devon, is served by three churches and a chapel.

A prized feature of St Michael's is the ring of eight bells ("the finest anywhere") hung in the "new" tower in 1897. Their overhaul was completed in 1993.

ST EDMUND'S, EXE BRIDGE

SEEN daily by thousands from traffic using Exe Bridge, a ruined tower is all that remains of St Edmund's, Exeter, which once stood at the end of a mediaeval bridge. A few 12th-century arches of the bridge, carefully restored, are still visible at the foundations of the old church.

When Western Way was developed in the 1960s, the building became redundant, but was made safe by removing dangerous stonework and a shell retained as a memorial of former times.

St Edmund-by-the-Bridge, as it was known over the centuries, was the original chapel on the first stone bridge built at that point around 1190.

Passing diagonally from the St Thomas side and leading up to the West Gate of the city by Stepcote Hill, the old bridge crossed not only the Exe but the marsh outside the city walls, and was about four times longer than the present bridge.

The dedication to St Edmund (849–870), the King whose shrine at Bury-St-Edmunds was famous all over Europe, gives credence to the belief that there was also a Saxon church here at the site of an earlier bridge crossing the river from at least Roman times. St Edmund's name was often given to similar chapels, as he was reputed to have taken refuge under a bridge after the Battle of Home. The body of Walter Gervase, Mayor of Exeter in 1231 and 1239, who built the mediaeval bridge, stayed in a chantry chapel until 1833, when it was buried beside the church.

The rector instituted by Bishop Bronescombe in 1259, John de Ponte, took his name from the new structure. Some of his living was taken in tithes of fish caught in the Exe.

Devon historian W. G. Hoskins records that John Williams, rector from 1554 to 1572, may well have set up Exeter's first printing press, for which he is thought to have brought equipment from Tavistock Abbey, where he had been a monk until it was dissolved in 1539.

An early "parishioner" was a holy woman who set up home on the bridge, often blocking traffic, but remained there for years, apparently because the authorities held her in superstitious awe.

During the Commonwealth St Edmund's was one of the four Exeter churches permitted by the Roundheads to take services.

In the Bishop's Census of 1744, Rector William Barter reported that his parish contained between 300 and 400 families, including "not more than five or six families of Dissenters of any kind."

In the 18th century a change in direction of Fore Street meant that the church no longer stood beside the main stream of traffic entering the city.

In 1800 the tower was struck by lightning, and extensive repairs were eventually carried out in 1833.

ST IDA'S, IDE

CHRISTIAN worship has been offered in a quiet corner of Ide, on the Western boundary of Exeter, at least since around 1050, when Leofric placed a church there amid lands he owned as Bishop of Exeter.

Leofric was once described as one who "went about his diocese, studiously preaching the word of God ... and building churches."

The last diocesan Bishop of Crediton from 1046 to 1050, he moved to the walled city of Exeter in 1050 to be personally installed as the first Bishop of Exeter by King Edward the Confessor.

Leofric made a present "for time immemorial" of the manor of Ide and its church to the Dean and Chapter of Exeter Cathedral. True to the spirit of the gift, the Cathedral remains patron of the parish to this day.

The dedication of the church to St Ida is unique in England. It is generally agreed that the saint, who lived in the 9th century, was a widow of one of Charlemagne's courtiers.

Another theory that the name Ida (and Ide) came from a 6th-century St Ita, Abbess of Limerick, who visited the south-west, has been discounted because there is no evidence of ancient British settlement locally.

Of the church built on the site in the 14th century, only the tower and the original nave foundations remain.

The church was staffed by vicars from the Cathedral during mediaeval times, and a gap in the list between 1450 and 1590 may be filled by a record that two vicars successively held office over a span of 121 years, one for 65, the other 56 years.

Further proof that Ide air is indeed healthy is provided by a register entry: "Dorothy Taylor was buried the 16th day of January 1608. She was by common report above 108 years of age. She was brought up in the Nunnery of Cornworthy and was the mother of 18 children."

Upheaval after the Civil War is revealed in another record that Vicar Robert Gaylord was obliged to have his marriage performed to Marie Tanton, widow, in 1654, not by a fellow clergyman, but by a Justice of the Peace.

William Satterley, thought to have been ejected as vicar by the Roundheads, resumed his post from 1665 to 1671.

Beatrix Cresswell identified shields of arms in the church as belonging to King Edward the Confessor and a succession of Bishops of Exeter from Leofric to Henry Phillpotts (1830–1855).

The dilapidated main body of the church was rebuilt in 1838 while the Rev. J. H. Earle was vicar (1832–55). The font he gave is of modern Gothic style and has 23 Greek letters carved in a palindrome (a line which reads the same both backwards and forwards). Its import is the washing away of evil.

The palindrome is one of 27 written by Leo Sapiens, Christian Emperor of Constantinople 886–911, and is inscribed in the vast Cathedral of St Sophia, now a museum.

ST MICHAEL'S, SOWTON

AS THE busy hum of daily traffic in Exeter's newest industrial estate subsides, the bells of the nearby parish church strike the peaceful evening air. How Sowton's noble ring of eight not six bells, as in most rural churches, has just been restored is a story of enterprise which could ring a message to many firms now occupying the "developed" half of the parish.

Sowton village, with a small population and the Church of St Michael and All Angels in its midst, is still well cushioned by farmland from the commercial scene on its west side.

Because of structural faults in the tower, however, the church bells were silent for 25 years, and churchwardens Dr "Barney" Alcock, who lives in the Old Rectory, and Farmer Fred Willmington decided they should be repaired. The first quotation of £20,000 was out of the question. So another estimate was obtained from Andrew Nicholson, of Lyme Regis. He quoted £4,500, provided he was helped by volunteers. Mr Willmington found seven willing helpers and Dr Alcock appealed for cash. Within three months the village raised £2,700, and grants from trusts made up the rest, including one which stipulated that the church was not "too high"! Their efforts were crowned in 1993, when before a packed church Rector Trevor Woodbridge re-dedicated the bells, which were rung with enthusiasm.

Sowton has had three names in the last 1,000 years – Clyst Fomison after the mediaeval Lord of the Manor, and later Clyst St Michael (after the church); its present unique name came about in 1541, when two gentlemen farmers, Stephen and John Sowton, founded the village. In 1983 two descendants, Philip and Edward Sowton, took over a restaurant in Topsham.

Sowton parish goes well beyond the village, covering three original farms Greatmoor, Middlemoor, and Littlemoor, and half of Clyst St Mary village. A green lane connects Sowton with Bishop's Clyst, the parish's greatest house, standing on a steep hill above the Clyst and surrounded by tall trees, daffodils, bluebells, and giant rhododendrons.

To pay debts to Jews, perhaps incurred during the Crusades, the Sackvilles sold the manor to Walter Bronescombe, Bishop of Exeter, in 1265, and it remained the bishops' summer palace until 1545. Some residents still believed the tale that there was a tunnel linking the manor and Cathedral Close. Until recently Bishops of Exeter have by custom spent the night before their enthronement in Sowton parish.

When in 1832 John Garratt, tea merchant and former Lord Mayor of London, bought Bishop's Clyst, he restored the derelict church and installed the eight bells.

George Barnes (rector 1826–47), who was also Archdeacon of Barnstaple, gave one of the old church bells to Bishop's Court, where it is still rung in the dark and lofty mediaeval chapel, well preserved by recent owners Taylor's paint firm. The 14th-century bell's Latin inscription is translated: "People all rejoice the more they hear me." Mrs Mary Carnall, of Clyst Honiton, on the staff of Taylor's firm, was one of those who believed that the chapel is haunted.

Col Lawrence Garratt held a tight grip on parish affairs until he died in 1946 – no "pub", telephone, or shop was allowed. The first phone was installed when the Alcocks, both doctors, came to the Old Rectory in 1948. As a hobby, Dr Nat. Alcock, of Warwick (Dr Barney's son) made a remarkable survey of all the ancient parish buildings which is now used for reference by national experts in this field.

The church itself has a pillar with the Tudor rose and pomegranate of Aragon carved at the time of Henry VIII's first marriage, and some odd grotesque faces are on the protected north wall.

In 1978 the church celebrated with Bishop Wilfrid Westall the 700 years since the appointment of Nicholas Strange as the first recorded rector by Bishop Bronescombe. There is good reason to look forward to another 700 years in the timeless side of Sowton.

ST MICHAEL'S, PINHOE

STANDING on a hill above the village, St Michael's, Pinhoe, gives a magnificent view of the Exe Estuary. It could have been from here that the unnamed priest first saw a Danish force landing in the year 1002.

After being repelled from the walls of Exeter, the Danes turned to meet a combined Devon and Somerset Army at Pinhoe. When the cry went up from the English for ammunition, it was the priest who ran to Exeter and fetched a supply of arrows.

Although the Danes won the battle and burned Pinhoe village, their plan to take Exeter was frustrated, and the brave priest was rewarded with an annual grant of one mark.

The Crown continued the yearly payment to Pinhoe rectors up to recent times, with the value reduced finally to 80p.

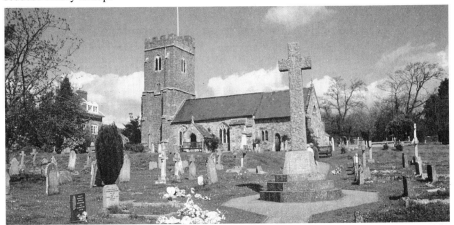

The present church, built in the 15th century, has a beautifully carved screen and pulpit. Evidence of earlier buildings on the site is the Norman font which is believed to have a Saxon base.

The fine old stone preaching cross in the churchyard, buried to escape desecration in the Civil War, was dug up and re-erected last century.

Bible Sunday is significant because John Reynolds, D.D., son of a Pinhoe rector and baptised here in 1549, led the scholars who translated the books of the prophets for the Authorised Version of the Bible in 1604.

As President of Corpus Christi College, Oxford, he was also tutor of Richard Hooker, of Heavitree, the great Anglican theologian, whose statue is in the Exeter Cathedral Close.

A memorial to Reynolds' memory is on the north wall. Another in the central aisle names John Land, founder of a parish charity, and proprietor of the New London Inn, Exeter, which he built in 1794.

W. G. Hoskins writes that it was not only the most important inn in the city, "but a centre of social political life throughout the 19th century."

When the wealthy innkeeper died in 1817, the funeral procession from Exeter to Pinhoe was a quarter-mile long and included a hearse with six horses, eight stage coaches with four horses each, 20 post chaises, and 200 men on horseback.

Pinhoe's most eccentric vicar, Oliver Puckridge, who held office for 40 years until 1942, is still fondly remembered. In a sentimental mood, he buried a pet donkey upright in the churchyard, and for a time its ears protruded from the ground.

He made trips to the visitors' gallery in Parliament, to shout protests at having to pay tax on the nominal 13s 2d paid to the successors of the arrow-fetching priest of 1002.

Absent-minded Bishop Lord William Cecil once asked after his wife and was told she had been dead some years. An hour later the bishop asked the same question. "Still dead," the rector replied. Latterly the Poltimore rector was often available when Puckridge forgot weddings or funerals.